8/12

W9-CFQ-104

TENNIS

BY MARTY GITLIN

CONTENT CONSULTANT
RANDY WALKER, TENNIS HISTORIAN

Published by ABDO Publishing Company, PO Box 398166, Minneapolis, Minnesota 55439. Copyright © 2012 by Abdo Consulting Group, Inc. International copyrights reserved in all countries. No part of this book may be reproduced in any form without written permission from the publisher. SportsZone™ is a trademark and logo of ABDO Publishing Company.

Printed in the United States of America,
North Mankato, Minnesota
102011
012012

Editor: Chrös McDougall
Copy Editor: Seth Putnam
Design and Production: Craig Hinton

Content Consultant: Randy Walker, tennis historian

Photo Credits: John Walton/Press Association/AP Images, cover (bottom); Dustin Steller/ iStockphoto, cover (top); AP Images, 1, 5, 13, 14, 24, 27, 30, 37, 38, 58 (middle), 58 (bottom); Ed Kolenovsky/AP Images, 6; Blair Pittman/AP Images, 10; Popperfoto/Getty Images, 17, 58 (top); AELTC/Tom Lovelock/AFP/Getty Images, 21; Harry Harris/AP Images, 34, 59 (top); Ronald C. Modra/Sports Imagery/Getty Images, 40; Adam Stoltman/AP Images, 43, 45, 59 (middle); Thomas Kienzle/AP Images, 47; Anja Niedringhaus/AP Images, 50; Ian Walton/AP Images, 52; Lionel Cironneau/AP Images, 56, 59 (bottom)

Library of Congress Cataloging-in-Publication Data
Gitlin, Marty.
 Tennis / by Marty Gitlin.
     p. cm. -- (Best sport ever)
 Includes index.
 ISBN 978-1-61783-147-8
 1. Tennis--Juvenile literature. I. Title.
 GV996.5.G58 2012
 796.342--dc23

                    2011033253

TABLE of CONTENTS

CHAPTER 1

BATTLE OF THE SEXES

A night many Americans had eagerly awaited finally arrived. It was September 20, 1973. A crowd of approximately 30,000 settled into their seats at the Houston Astrodome. An estimated 40 million more prepared to watch at home on television. The Battle of the Sexes was about to begin.

This was not just a tennis match. It was an event. Tennis was beginning a period of tremendous growth. In 1968, the biggest tennis tournaments began allowing professional players to compete in them. That helped the game's biggest stars get even more global exposure. So when Billie Jean King agreed to face off against Bobby Riggs, their Battle of the Sexes instantly became one of the most anticipated tennis matches ever.

Billie Jean King, *left*, and Bobby Riggs answer questions at a press conference prior to their 1973 Battle of the Sexes.

Bobby Riggs confidently strolls down a sidewalk in Houston, Texas, with two female fans prior to his 1973 Battle of the Sexes against Billie Jean King.

On that fateful day in 1973, King and Riggs introduced millions of people to the excitement of tennis. They also played a major role in advancing women's rights, both in sports and society.

The Matchup

The 29-year-old King was the finest female tennis player in the world at the time. The 55-year-old Riggs, a former champion himself, had boasted for months that he could defeat any woman. And to some extent he had backed it up. Riggs had dominated top women's player Margaret Smith Court just four months earlier.

So lopsided was Riggs's victory over Court in May that it became forever known as the Mother's Day Massacre. King had warned Court before that match that she needed to beat Riggs. The honor of women everywhere was at stake. King was furious when she learned Riggs had clobbered Court. She knew at that point that she had to play Riggs herself. And she knew that she had to win.

King's challenge of Riggs came at an important time for women in the United States. Women were seeking and pushing for equality in all walks of American life. Even in tennis tournaments, the female players were demanding equal prize money. The Battle of the Sexes was symbolic of those struggles.

"I thought it would set us back 50 years if I didn't win that match," King said. "It would ruin the women's tour and affect all women's self-esteem."

Title IX

King wasn't just fighting for women's equality in society and tennis when she played Riggs. She was also fighting for Title IX. Title IX is a 1972 bill that sought equal funding for girls and women's amateur sports. Before that time, boys' and men's high school and college athletic programs received more money.

King was successful in promoting that cause. President Gerald Ford signed Title IX

KING OF THE COURT

Billie Jean King became a star well before the celebrated Battle of the Sexes match. She became a legend after it. King won 10 Grand Slam singles titles before her match against Bobby Riggs, including Wimbledon, the US Open, and the French Open in 1972. That year she became the first tennis player and the first female to be named *Sports Illustrated* magazine's Sportsman of the Year.

She continued to win after beating Riggs. King snagged the US Open crown in 1974 and the Wimbledon championship a year later. In 1987, she was elected into the International Tennis Hall of Fame.

Life Magazine placed King on its list of the 100 Most Important Americans of the Twentieth Century in 1990. And in 2006, the United States National Tennis Center was renamed the Billie Jean King National Tennis Center.

into law in 1975. It was an event that drastically increased opportunities for girls and women to play sports.

The Show Begins

The Battle of the Sexes pitted man against woman even before the first serve was smashed. King was carried in on a gold chariot by five muscular men wearing togas. Riggs was taken in on a rickshaw pulled by six female models who were wearing tight outfits. It seemed everyone in the country had a favorite. They were all rooting with passion for either King or Riggs.

King had a plan. Riggs had frustrated Court by changing speeds on the ball and using trickery. He used drop shots that barely fell over the net, and Court could not reach them. King wanted to first tire Riggs out by moving him around the court. Then she would overpower the older player and attack the net.

Billie Jean King enters the Houston Astrodome atop a chariot held up by five muscular men for the highly anticipated Battle of the Sexes.

Riggs started out strong, taking a 3–2 lead in the first set. So King began placing the ball softly from one side of the court to the other. She was making Riggs run. Soon he was drenched in sweat. King won four of the next five games and the set, 6–4.

King was in control. She began to attack the net to volley. As Riggs became weaker, so did his shots. He tried to lob the ball over King's head, but his shots fell short and she slammed them for overhead winners. He attempted to smack shots past her, but she reached them and angled the ball away from him.

Riggs managed to break King's serve to start the second set, but King broke right back. In tennis, a player who wins a game in which he or she is not serving breaks the opponent's serve. King looked strong and confident. She hit hard shots deep in the court. Riggs appeared to be every bit of his 55 years. He reached in vain as King's forehands and backhands whizzed by. King won the second set, 6–3.

The End for Riggs

Even many King fans began to feel sorry for Riggs. He had entertained the media and millions of Americans with his sense of humor leading up to the match. He had purposely played the role of a rude, sexist man to help build up the Battle of the Sexes.

HEAVY METAL

A revolution in tennis equipment was launched in the early 1970s. Racket frames previously had been made with wood. The first manufacturer of metal rackets was Wilson, which introduced the T-2000. The racket gained fame when US men's star Jimmy Connors began to use it. By the late 1970s, nearly all the professional players had switched from wood to metal rackets.

But he was not laughing now. He looked defeated physically and emotionally. His determination and confidence seemed to be gone. He felt cramps in his hand.

The match was not done, but Riggs was. And when it was over, King had earned a 6–4, 6–3, 6–3 victory. She had avenged Court's defeat and brought honor to the women's game. More importantly, King had given a greater sense of pride and strength to the women's movement in front of the entire nation. *Sports Illustrated* writer Curry Kirkpatrick understood the significance of King's achievement. He also marveled at how well she played despite the pressure of carrying a torch for women everywhere:

> *On King's part it was a brilliant rising to an occasion, a clutch performance under the most trying of circumstances. Seldom has there been a more classic example of a skilled athlete performing at peak efficiency in the most important moment of her life.*

Thousands came out to the Houston Astrodome to cheer on Billie Jean King or Bobby Riggs at the Battle of the Sexes.

Billie Jean King's victory over Bobby Riggs in the Battle of the Sexes brought worldwide attention to tennis and helped showcase women's sports.

At the Battle of the Sexes, fans saw more than just an exciting tennis match. The sport had long been known as a rich man's game. With growing acceptance of women and a new generation of diverse players, tennis was about to embark on its golden era.

Friends at Last

The perception of Riggs changed with time. It became clear he was more of a hustler than one who believed men were superior to women. He believed he could gain fame and fortune by challenging King to the Battle of the Sexes. And he was right.

King eventually became friends with Riggs. And when Riggs was on his deathbed in 1995, King phoned him. She told him the Battle of the Sexes was not only his greatest hustle. She reminded him that he had played a role in the fight for women's equality. Then she told him one more thing.

"I love you," King said.

"I love you," Riggs replied. "Well, we did it. We really made a difference, didn't we?"

CHAPTER 2

WHERE IT BEGAN: WHO KNOWS?

Nobody knows exactly who invented tennis nor when it came to be. Several theories exist, however. There is evidence that a form of the sport was played thousands of years ago in ancient Greece. Others claim that it truly began in twelfth-century France. Tennis can at least be traced back that far. However, it was first played with a wooden ball and no racket. The game was an offshoot of what we know today as handball.

The sport had grown in popularity by the fourteenth century, particularly among European monks. However, it was soon considered a game only for royal families and the wealthy. England's King Henry VIII had a court built at his Hampton Court Palace residence in the 1530s. The racket was invented

Twin brothers William and Ernest Renshaw won five doubles championships and a combined eight singles championships at Wimbledon during the 1880s.

THE FOUR MUSKETEERS

Four of the finest players of the 1920s emerged from France. Jean Borotra, René Lacoste, Henri Cochet, and Jacques Brugnon were known as the Four Musketeers. But they did not always get along.

"They were all very different in style and temperament," wrote Wimbledon secretary Duncan Macaulay. "And they sometimes clashed bitterly with one another on the courts. But whenever they felt they were playing for France . . . they always put France first."

Brugnon was a doubles specialist, but the other Musketeers took turns beating each other from 1924 to 1932. Lacoste won two Wimbledons, two US Championships, and three French Championships during that time. Cochet won two Wimbledons and four French Championships. Borotra captured two Wimbledon titles.

The French have remained major players in the sport but have never matched their success of the 1920s. Countryman Yannick Noah did win the French Open in 1983.

in Italy later that century. But the popularity of tennis had not spread beyond European nobility. It was especially embraced by French noblemen. The reputation of tennis as a rich person's game did not change for centuries.

It remained in 1873, when British major Walter Wingfield invented a lawn version of the sport. He called it *Sphairistikè*, which is translated from Greek to mean "ball game." It more closely resembled the sport that tennis is known to be today, though the court was shorter and shaped like an hourglass. Wingfield's game featured rackets, a rubber ball, and a net in the middle tied to two posts.

A year later, an American named Mary Outerbridge saw

British army officers playing tennis while on vacation in Bermuda. She brought some equipment home and began teaching others how to play. She is known today as the "Mother of American Tennis." Tennis also spread to other countries around this time, such as Russia, China, India, and Canada. Before long, it was truly a global game.

Beginning of the Grand Slams

Soon the top players were spotlighted in events that still entertain millions to this day. The most famous and admired tournament is the Wimbledon Championships. That annual tournament was established in 1877 and is still played at the All England Lawn Tennis Club. Wimbledon rests in a south suburb of London, England.

Other prestigious tournaments followed. The United States Championships (now the US Open) was first played in 1881. The French Championships (now the French Open) was established in 1891. The Australasian Championships (later the Australian Championships and now the Australian Open) began in 1905.

Entry into such events was limited in the early years to players from those countries. Each nation boasted its own tennis

SMASHING!

What made the British Renshaw brothers two of the greatest players of their time? They developed and used the overhead smash. The overhead is generally hit from near the net. It is used when the contact point with the ball is higher than shoulder level. You must watch the ball closely. Take the racket head over your head, and then place it toward your back. Strike the ball with the racket just past its peak height. Hit it down toward the other end of the court with great force. Try to angle it away from your opponent.

stars. The Wimbledon men's event was dominated by twin brothers William and Ernest Renshaw. They combined to win 13 singles and doubles championships from 1881 to 1889. During that same era, Richard Sears captured seven consecutive US Championships titles.

Tennis was recognized worldwide in 1896 when it was included in the first modern Olympic Games. The Davis Cup began in 1900 as a competition between US and British players. It eventually grew into a tournament involving the top stars from many nations. The International Lawn Tennis Federation was created in 1912. Its purpose was to coordinate the four major tennis championships. It combined Wimbledon, the French Open, the US Open, and what became known as the Australian Open to form the Grand Slam of tennis.

The All England Lawn Tennis and Croquet Club has hosted the Wimbledon Championships since 1877. It is the oldest of the Grand Slams.

The sport did not thrive until after the premier players in the world began participating in events outside their countries, following the end of World War I in 1918. The two decades following the war were considered the first golden era of tennis.

Female stars such as Suzanne Lenglen and Helen Wills Moody won title after title while Bill Tilden dominated the men's game.

Match with More Meaning

The importance of tennis triumphs did not usually extend beyond the court. One Davis Cup match in 1937 took on far greater meaning. It pitted US champion Don Budge against German Gottfried von Cramm. At the time, dictator Adolf Hitler and his Nazi Party ruled Germany. The Nazis would soon start World War II, resulting in the deaths of 50 million people.

Hitler had convinced many Germans that they were superior to all other races. He wanted German athletes and teams to prove they were the best. Hitler called Von Cramm before the match and warned him that he needed to win.

The German tennis star did not like Hitler or the Nazis, partly because of their hatred for Jewish people. Von Cramm had already angered the Nazis by protesting when they kicked Jewish player Daniel Prenn off Germany's Davis Cup team. Von Cramm felt plenty of pressure after hearing from Hitler.

"Gottfried came out pale and serious and played as if his life depended on every point," Budge recalled.

The German rose to the occasion by winning the first two sets. Budge answered by taking the next two, but he fell behind 4–1 in the fifth and deciding set. Budge grew desperate. He began attacking the net after returning Von Cramm's serve.

The strategy worked. Budge forged ahead, 7–6. Von Cramm battled gamely. He fought off five match points that could have sealed his defeat. But Budge won his sixth attempt at match point with a diving, sprawling shot. His thrilling win gave the United States a victory over Germany in the Davis Cup. It is still considered one of the greatest matches in tennis history.

"Don, this was absolutely the finest match I have ever played in my life," Von Cramm said as he shook Budge's hand at the net. "I'm very happy I could have played it against you, whom I like so much. Congratulations."

Don Budge returns a shot against Gottfried von Cramm during the men's final at Wimbledon in 1937.

THE WIGHTMAN CUP

Hazel Hotchkiss Wightman believed in the early 1920s that women should have their own international event. After all, the men had the Davis Cup. So Wightman donated a sterling vase as a prize for what became known as the Wightman Cup. The annual tournament between the best US and British female players began in 1923. The Wightman Cup was played through 1989. The US women dominated, winning 51 of 61 tournaments. Today, the Fed Cup pits women's national teams from around the world against each other.

The two players embraced. "I think we both wanted to cry," Budge said later.

The Nazis arrested Von Cramm and sent him to jail one year later, in 1938, after he criticized the German government. He later fought for Germany in the Soviet Union during World War II. But he was not one of the millions of Germans who died on that front.

Von Cramm survived the war and even played at Wimbledon at age 42 in 1951. By that time, however, a new generation of stars was bringing excitement to the sport.

CHAPTER 3

BATTLES ON AND OFF THE COURT

T he United States has long been called a "melting pot." Millions of immigrants came ashore from Europe and Asia in the late 1800s and early 1900s. They sought freedom and prosperity while bringing great diversity to the country.

There was little diversity in tennis, though. The top players were almost all white and wealthy well into the twentieth century. Many were introduced to the sport at country clubs and taught by private instructors. There were few opportunities for middle- and lower-class people to participate.

The Great Depression hit the United States during the 1930s. Most Americans were concerned about finding work or even their next meal. They could not afford to join

Known for her flamboyant dresses and headbands, French star Suzanne Lenglen won six Wimbledon titles as an amateur between 1919 and 1926.

DIFFERENT COURTS, DIFFERENT SURFACES

Every Grand Slam event presents unique challenges. That is because of the various court surfaces on which the players compete. The French Open, for instance, is played on clay. The ball bounces higher on clay and gives the players more time to set up their shots. Players with powerful serves and aggressive net games are often frustrated by the slow play. The clay surface favors baseline players. One tactic often used on clay is the drop shot, which is hit softly just over the net. If placed well, drop shots cannot be reached by opponents on the opposite baseline.

Wimbledon is played on grass. It is the fastest surface among those at Grand Slam sites. The grass surface benefits players with powerful serves. Opponents have a hard time getting their racket prepared to hit speedy serves on grass. The US Open and Australian Open are played on hard-court surfaces. Shots move much faster than they do on clay, but not as quickly as they do on grass. Hard courts still favor power players.

country clubs or pay for tennis lessons, even after the Great Depression ended. Immigrants and African Americans, who had been discriminated against for generations, were particularly poor. Those in rural areas and small towns also struggled. In fact, only a few Americans had enough money to become great in tennis.

Although it often took a lot of money to fund a top tennis career, there was not a lot of money to be earned through tennis. The tournaments were for amateurs only. Amateurs are not allowed to earn money for playing. At the time, events such as Wimbledon and the US Championships provided no prize money. Promoters sometimes paid players to compete in exhibition matches. But if players accepted that money, they would become professionals and no longer be allowed to participate in amateur events against the best players in the world.

That caused a problem. Tennis stars especially wanted to play in the major tournaments. They yearned to earn a rare Grand Slam by winning all four in the same year, as Don Budge did in 1938. But they also wanted to earn money for their work.

The First Pro Stars

Players became angry and frustrated. US promoter Charles "C. C." Pyle had already launched the first professional tour in 1926. He signed Wimbledon winner Suzanne Lenglen, as well as 1924 Olympic men's champion Vinnie Richards. Other US and French stars joined them on a tour of the United States and Canada. The players made thousands of dollars but could no longer compete in events such as Wimbledon.

By the late 1940s, stars such as Budge, Bobby Riggs, Frank Parker, Jack Kramer, and Pancho Gonzalez had all turned professional. The lack of amateur players during that era did not allow any one player to dominate the Grand Slam events.

The only two women to rise above the rest just before and after World War II were Americans Alice Marble and Maureen

Althea Gibson was the first black player to win the singles title at the French, US, and Wimbledon championships. She dominated during the late 1950s.

THE OFFENSIVE LOB

Australian champion Ken Rosewall boasted one of the best lobs ever. Lobbing can be a great weapon, but it takes precision and touch. When done well, it can frustrate opponents at the net. The key is to lob the ball just over the opponent's reach. If it is hit too high, he or she will have enough time to race back and reach it. If it is hit too short, he or she can smash it for a winner. The lob should be struck hard enough to hit near the baseline. That way, the opponent will be less likely to reach the ball and return it effectively.

"Little Mo" Connolly. Marble overpowered opponents with her serve-and-volley game and dominated the sport in the late 1930s. Connolly blasted away from the baseline with hard forehands and backhands, which are also called ground strokes. In 1953, she became the first woman to win a Grand Slam by sweeping all four major events.

Australians took over men's tennis in the 1950s. Frank Sedgman began the run of Australian dominance in the early 1950s. The male stars of that country ruled the game over the next two decades. Sedgman was followed by champions such as Ashley Cooper, Ken Rosewall, Lew Hoad, Neale Fraser, Rod Laver, Roy Emerson, and John Newcombe.

Tennis changed very little from the end of World War II in the 1940s into the late 1960s. It was still largely considered a rich, white person's game. One of the exceptions was African-American female star Althea Gibson. The growing number of public courts built after the war gave millions of Americans a chance to play for the first time. Gibson took advantage of that opportunity and blossomed. She won five Grand Slam events from 1956 to 1958.

Those same tournaments continued to lose credibility as more players turned professional, however. Australian stars Rosewall and Laver joined the pro ranks in the 1960s. Finally, in 1968, the International Lawn Tennis Federation announced that professional players could compete in all events. That began what is now known as the Open Era. The French Championships were the first to go open, or allow both amateurs and professionals. It became called the French Open. The other

"JACK" OF ALL TRADES

Jack Kramer did everything well in regard to tennis. He was the top-ranked player in the world in 1946 and 1947. After turning pro, he played a series of exhibitions against Bobby Riggs and won 69 of their 89 matches. Kramer later became a tennis promoter before helping form the Association of Tennis Professionals (ATP) in 1972. It began as a players' union for male tennis players. He then served as an expert on tennis broadcasts on television for more than 20 years.

Grand Slams soon followed. By the early 1970s, almost all of the top players had become professionals.

The Greatest Aussie of All

Laver was the finest player in the group of top Australians—and perhaps the greatest player in tennis history. He twice won all four majors in the same year, thereby capturing the Grand Slam in 1962 and 1969. The brilliant left-hander remained the last male player to achieve that feat through 2011.

The 1962 French Championships were the most dramatic. Laver lost the first two sets of the finals to Emerson before winning the next three and the title. He clinched his second Grand Slam by beating fellow Australian Tony Roche in the 1969 US Open final. The tennis world marveled at the accomplishment. Laver won 17 of 32 tournaments that season and finished the year with a 106–16 record.

One *Sports Illustrated* writer expressed his disbelief at what Laver had achieved after the easy victory over Roche.

"It looks as though the sport will have to be opened considerably wider, to include angels, highly trained kangaroos, or something yet [unseen] before anyone else will be in Laver's league," he wrote.

Australian superstar Rod Laver follows through with his shot during the 1969 US Open. He won his second Grand Slam that year.

The same could be said for another Australian named Margaret Smith Court. She won all seven Australian Championships from 1960 to 1966 and four more Australian Opens between 1969 and 1973. She also won seven US Opens, three Wimbledons, and five French Opens. In 1970 Court matched Laver by capturing all four majors for a Grand Slam.

Players such as Laver and Court faced many strong opponents in the 1960s and early 1970s, but the move to open the sport to professional players greatly raised the level of competition. Young men and women were about to take the game by storm. The 1973 Battle of the Sexes between Billie Jean King and Bobby Riggs ignited an explosion of tennis popularity. The sport was about to enter its greatest era.

CHAPTER 4

THE GOLDEN ERA OF TENNIS

Tennis has been called a "gentleman's game." Throughout the game's history, players have generally showed a pleasant demeanor and good sportsmanship on the court. But some believed the sport lacked personality because players were discouraged from showing their emotions.

All that changed in the 1970s, particularly in men's tennis. The premier players in the world had no problems displaying their anger and frustration on the court. They yelled at the lines judges, who were responsible for calling shots in or out. They yelled at the umpires who tried to maintain control of the match. They yelled at each other. They even yelled at themselves.

Ilie Năstase argues with fans at the 1979 US Open. That type of loud behavior had previously been unheard of in tennis, but fans could not get enough.

Americans Jimmy Connors, *left*, and Chris Evert show off their Wimbledon singles trophies in 1974.

The first "bad boy" of tennis was "Nasty" Ilie Năstase. The quick, athletic Năstase was among the game's best players. He was even ranked number one in the world in 1973. The Romanian entertained fans with his antics, but he also angered officials and opponents. He glared, mocked, and taunted them. And he was often fined or suspended for his behavior.

Năstase scorned US opponent Cliff Richey, insulting his performance by making animal noises at him. He threw a towel at a line judge, and then was booed for making an obscene gesture to the crowd. He twice slammed balls into the back of a female foe in a mixed doubles match. He ridiculed opponent Clark Graebner so terribly that the American jumped over the net, grabbed Năstase by the shirt and threatened to hit him over the head with his racket.

"I am a little crazy," Năstase said, "but I try to be a good boy."

More Stars

Năstase and other popular and talented young stars increased excitement for tennis and created memorable rivalries. Among the new players who emerged in the early 1970s were US stars Jimmy Connors and Chris Evert. They both quickly rose to number one in the rankings. They also started dating each other. They won tournament after tournament and revolutionized tennis by using two-handed backhands. Until the 1970s, almost all players gripped their backhands with only one hand. Today nearly everyone uses two.

TWO-HANDED BACKHAND

Not only were Chris Evert and Jimmy Connors a couple in the early 1970s, they also popularized the two-handed backhand. Many believe a two-handed stroke provides greater power and control. The second hand is placed on top with the palm facing parallel to the court. The follow-through of that arm allows you to aim the ball where you want it. Using two arms to hit the ball also adds power to the stroke.

Martina Navratilova sets up to blast a forehand back across the net during a 1986 Fed Cup match in Czechoslovakia.

Other stars burst through as well. Masterful Swede Björn Borg remained mostly on the baseline and frustrated foes by placing his shots where they could not be reached. Czechoslovakian Martina Navratilova dominated with her power. She attacked the net and destroyed opponents quickly. She was the top-ranked player in the world for five years during the 1980s.

Fans eagerly awaited Grand Slam showdowns between the top players. It seemed each star owned one or two events in the 1970s and early 1980s. Connors won five US Open titles. Borg won five Wimbledon titles and six French Open titles. Evert snagged the French Open title seven times and added six US Open championships. Navratilova won six straight Wimbledon titles from 1982 to 1987 and nine altogether. She is regarded as one of the greatest female players in tennis history.

The "Super Brat" of Tennis

Another loud but talented tennis player emerged in the late 1970s. John McEnroe of the United States was one of the top players in the world throughout the 1980s, winning the US Open four times and Wimbledon three times. But he was equally notorious for throwing tantrums on the court.

Perhaps his most famous outburst occurred at Wimbledon in 1981. Angry over a line call, he banged his chair with his racket. When another call went against him, McEnroe screamed at the umpire.

"Man, you cannot be serious!" he shrieked. The rant ended with McEnroe shouting, "You guys are the absolute pits of the world, you know that?"

GREAT PLAYER, GREAT MAN

Arthur Ashe learned to play tennis as a child in Richmond, Virginia, during a time of racial segregation. As an African American, he was not allowed to play against whites in youth tournaments. But with his calm demeanor and respectful approach to the game, Ashe was able to succeed. He went on to win the 1965 college national championship, the 1968 US Open, and the 1970 Australian Open. Perhaps his biggest victory was a shocking upset over Jimmy Connors in the 1975 Wimbledon final. That made Ashe the first African-American men's Wimbledon champion.

Ashe did not slow down after a heart attack ended his career in 1979. Known for his keen intelligence and strong moral character, Ashe stepped up his missions off the court. He strongly protested the policy of racial separation in South Africa. And after contracting the AIDS virus from a blood transfusion, Ashe worked to educate others about that disease. Ashe died from AIDS in 1993. In 1997, the main US Open venue in New York was named Arthur Ashe Stadium.

Players such as Năstase and McEnroe were roundly criticized for their behavior. While their behavior was not positive, the attention it garnered for the sport was. Relatively few Americans considered themselves passionate tennis fans before the 1970s. By the middle of the decade, public courts throughout the nation were filled with players learning the game.

The Finest Match Ever?

Perhaps no single match of that era was more exciting than the 1980 Wimbledon men's final between McEnroe and Borg. Borg, who had captured the last three Wimbledon titles, lost the first set. He fought back to win the next two, placing himself on the verge of another championship.

In a familiar scene, US tennis star John McEnroe argues a call with an official at the 1987 US Open.

The fourth set was tied at 6–6. That forced a tiebreaker— extra points played to determine the winner of a set. If Borg won the tiebreaker, he would win the match. But the tenacious McEnroe won five Borg match points. McEnroe eventually won the tiebreaker, 18–16, and forced a fifth set. Borg, however, was known for his ability to keep his composure. He never got rattled. He matched McEnroe shot for shot. He captured the fifth set, 8–6, and his fifth consecutive Wimbledon crown. Many still consider it the most epic tennis match ever played.

"You'd think after all these years I'd be sick and tired of the mention of it, but I'm not," McEnroe said in 2009. "It seems like I lost that match 20 times more than any other. Yet when you have a rivalry as good as ours it's an honor to know it's still remembered." McEnroe avenged that defeat by beating Borg in the 1981 Wimbledon final. But soon new tennis greats began laying claim to the titles of king and queen of the court.

Masterful Swede Björn Borg rejoices after defeating John McEnroe to win the 1980 Wimbledon men's singles championship.

CHAPTER 5

NEW GENERATIONS OF GREATNESS

Public courts in the United States were no longer jam-packed by the late 1980s. The popularity of the sport waned. The tennis boom was over. But in the next two decades, three exciting rivalries created tremendous interest in the United States and beyond.

The first peaked in the 1990s as Americans Pete Sampras and Andre Agassi dueled for supremacy. Sampras won 20 of the 34 matches they played against each other. Soon he was clearly established as the premier player in the world. Some believed he was the greatest player in the history of the sport. It was hard to argue after he swept Agassi in three sets to win the 1999 Wimbledon championship.

US tennis star Pete Sampras was known for his powerful serves as he won 14 Grand Slam titles in his career.

"That's probably the best I've played in many years," Sampras said. "I couldn't have played any better, pure and simple." Agassi chimed in, marveling that Sampras "walked on water."

Both players had great careers. Sampras won five US Opens and seven Wimbledon titles. When he retired in 2002, his 14 Grand Slam titles were the most of any male player. Early on, Agassi was known as much for his crazy haircut as he was for his great tennis play. But through the years he established himself as an American tennis icon. His best Grand Slam event was the Australian Open, which he captured four times.

The Great Graf

No tennis player was more dominant—perhaps ever— than German star Steffi Graf. She won all four majors in 1988, becoming the last player through 2011 to snag a Grand Slam in a calendar year. She also won an Olympic gold medal that year.

SHOCK FOR SELES

Monica Seles was the top-ranked women's player in 1993. She had already won two US Opens, three French Opens, and two Australian Opens. Everything changed on April 30 of that year. Seles was taking a breather during a match when a deranged German fan emerged from the stands. He stabbed Seles in the back with a 10-inch knife. Seles did not play again for two years. Remarkably, she returned to win the Australian Open in 1996.

That feat was dubbed the Golden Slam and had not been matched through the 2008 Olympic Games. Most remarkable is that she accomplished that rare feat before the age of 20. And she was just warming up. Graf finished her brilliant career with 22 Grand Slam event titles. Of both men and women, only Margaret Smith Court has more, with 24 Grand Slam victories.

Super Sisters

By the time Sampras and Agassi retired, another all-American rivalry had begun. This one was between two African-American sisters. Venus Williams and Serena Williams skyrocketed to the top of the tennis world in the early 2000s.

THE AGASSI FOUNDATION

Andre Agassi made millions of dollars during his tennis career. Since retiring, he has spent much of his time using his money to help struggling youth around the world. The Andre Agassi Charitable Foundation has focused on kids. In 1997, it donated $2 million to construct a six-room classroom building for abused and neglected children in Nevada. It also provided nearly $1 million for a facility that helped handicapped or diseased children. In 2001, Agassi launched a free school to prepare underprivileged kids for college. In 2007, he joined many others in starting Athletes for Hope, an organization to help professional athletes get involved in charity work.

Agassi married fellow tennis star Steffi Graf in 2001. Graf has also been deeply involved in charities for kids. She began a foundation called Children for Tomorrow. The organization was started to help kids who have been mentally or emotionally harmed through war or other disasters.

Sisters and doubles partners Serena Williams, *left*, and Venus Williams attack the net at Wimbledon in 2010.

Venus won the US Open and Wimbledon in 2000 and 2001. She won three more Wimbledon titles, but Serena eventually emerged as the more consistent champion. She captured all four Grand Slam events during her career. Including her first Grand Slam title in 1999, she won three US Opens, four Wimbledons, one French Open, and five Australian Opens through 2011. In 2002 they became the first siblings to hold the top two places on the world rankings.

Their two biggest competitors during the early 2000s were often Belgians Justine Henin and Kim Clijsters. Henin won seven Grand Slam tournaments and Clijsters won four through the 2011 season.

Still, the powerful Williams sisters were the faces of women's tennis throughout the early 2000s. However, having two talented sisters meant that they sometimes had to face each other in big matches. When Serena beat Venus in the 2009 Wimbledon final, it was their eighth time meeting in a Grand Slam final. For good measure, though, the Williams sisters have won 12 Grand Slam doubles titles together through 2011.

A New Men's Rivalry

After the turn of the twenty-first century, the retirements of Sampras and Agassi left the United States with few players contending for championships. Andy Roddick's 2003 win at the US Open was the last Grand Slam title for a US man through 2011. One reason US men struggled was because Swiss star Roger Federer and Spaniard Rafael Nadal were winning nearly all the Grand Slam events.

Tennis fans eagerly anticipated Federer-Nadal showdowns. Their playing styles contrasted greatly, making their matches

Roger Federer reaches for a return shot against Rafael Nadal during the 2008 Wimbledon final.

more intriguing. Like Björn Borg from a generation earlier, Nadal preferred to stay back at the baseline. He beat his opponents from there by angling his shots. He rarely made mistakes. Federer simply did everything well. But when he played Nadal, he tended to attack the net to keep his opponent from controlling the game.

That contrast was in full display at the 2008 Wimbledon final. Federer was seeking his sixth straight Wimbledon title. He had not lost on a grass court in six years. The young Nadal had yet to win any Grand Slam event other than the French Open, which he had won the past four years. That was where the slow clay court fit his game perfectly.

The two giants of tennis battled for nearly five hours in what many believe to be among the most intense matches ever. Nadal won the first two sets. No man since 1927 had won a Wimbledon

ANDY RODDICK

While Roger Federer and Rafael Nadal were dominating men's tennis during the early 2000s, Americans pinned their hopes on Andy Roddick. Roddick was the best US player of the decade. He owned the fastest serve in the game, but he was inconsistent. He won the US Open in 2003. Then he reached the finals at Wimbledon in 2004, 2005, and 2009 and at the US Open in 2006. However, through 2011 he has yet to claim another Grand Slam title.

final after losing the first two sets. But Federer set out to do just that. Mother Nature was not cooperating, though. Rain delayed the third set by more than an hour.

Fantastic Finish

Federer won the third and fourth sets in tiebreakers. He fended off two match points in the fourth-set tiebreaker before winning it on a backhand passing shot. He leaped for joy as 15,000 fans roared their approval.

The fifth set was tied at 7–7. Federer was serving—and neither player had lost a game while serving since the second set. But Nadal broke his serve. Then he won his own to capture the Wimbledon crown. When it was finally over, Nadal tossed his racket aside and threw himself onto his back in celebration.

"I am very happy for me, but sorry for [Federer] because he deserved this title, too," Nadal said.

Looking toward Tomorrow

Tennis has undergone many changes throughout its history. What began as a game played among nobility is now a sport that is played all around the world. The biggest competitions, such as the Grand Slam events, are watched by millions of people at the stadiums and on television.

After many years struggling to shed its identity as an elitist's game, tennis has become more accessible to all people over the past several decades. The Williams sisters are an example of that. They grew up in a poor area of Los Angeles, California, and occasionally had to endure discrimination from white opponents. But today they are among the biggest stars in the world, on and off the court. They entertain fans not only with their powerful ground strokes, but also with their flashy tennis outfits that they help design.

THE TOPSPIN FOREHAND

Nobody in modern tennis has boasted a more deadly topspin forehand than Rafael Nadal. His forehand jumped when it hit the court. The topspin is effective because it takes a quicker and higher bounce. It gives an opponent less time to prepare a return shot. It also helps get the ball to land within the boundaries of the court. It rises slightly as it approaches the net, then drops when it reaches the other side of the court.

To hit topspin, start the racket low. The racket head must loop slightly up and across as it meets the ball. The racket should then follow through to the opposite shoulder.

Rafael Nadal blasts a serve during a clay-court tournament in 2011. He won three of the four Grand Slam events in 2010.

For years, most tennis players were known for their modest demeanor. Stars of the 1970s and 1980s such as Jimmy Connors, John McEnroe, and Ilie Năstase brought great attention to the sport by being just the opposite. Today's players are not quite as loud or brash, but they are just as exciting.

The top players come from countries all around the world. In 2011, Li Na became the first Chinese player to reach the final of a Grand Slam when she did so at the Australian Open. Then she became the first Chinese player to win a Grand Slam when she won the 2011 French Open. On the men's side, Serbian Novak Djokovic began the 2011 season with 41 straight victories. That was one shy of McEnroe's Open Era-record of 42 straight victories to start 1984. Among Djokovic's wins was the Australian Open title. That summer he defeated Nadal to win his first Wimbledon title. Then he beat Nadal again to win his first US Open title. Many view Djokovic as the game's next big star.

Throughout its full history, tennis has seen many different eras. Unique stars have dominated the sport along the way. But as one generation gives way to the next, tennis has always shown the ability to generate new stars and to continue to grow. With the sport becoming more and more accessible to play and to watch, there is no telling how much more it can grow.

TIMELINE

1583	The first tennis racket is invented in Italy.
1873	British major Walter Wingfield invents *Sphairistikè*, a sport that resembles modern tennis.
1877	The first Wimbledon Championships begin on July 9. Brothers William and Ernest Renshaw dominate the early Wimbledon tournaments.
1881	The first US Championships is played in August in Rhode Island. It is known today as the US Open.
1891	The French Championships is established. The tournament is now known as the French Open.
1905	The tournament that would become the Australian Open begins and becomes the last of the four Grand Slam events.
1920	The International Lawn Tennis Federation is formed to coordinate the four Grand Slam events.
1926	American promoter Charles "C. C." Pyle launches the first tour for professional players.
1938	Don Budge becomes the first player to win all four major tournaments, thereby completing a Grand Slam.
1953	Maureen "Little Mo" Connolly wins all four major tournaments to earn the first women's Grand Slam.
1958	Althea Gibson becomes the first African American to win a Grand Slam event when she captures the French Championships.
1968	The International Lawn Tennis Federation announces that professional players can compete in all events. The Open Era begins.

1969 Rod Laver becomes the only player to twice win all four majors, thereby earning two Grand Slams.

1973 Billie Jean King wins the Battle of the Sexes on September 20 by beating Bobby Riggs in front of 30,000 fans at the Houston Astrodome in Texas.

1975 Arthur Ashe becomes the first African-American Wimbledon men's champion on July 5 when he upsets Jimmy Connors in the finals.

1980 Björn Borg wins his fifth consecutive Wimbledon title with an epic five-set victory over John McEnroe on July 5.

1986 The Women's Tennis Association ranks Martina Navratilova the number one player in the world for the fifth straight year. Chris Evert has been ranked second all five years.

1988 German Steffi Graf snags all four majors to win a rare Grand Slam. She becomes the last player—male or female—to win all four Grand Slam events in a calendar year through 2011.

1995 American rivals Pete Sampras and Andre Agassi meet twice in Grand Slam finals. Agassi wins the Australian Open on January 29, but Sampras earns revenge at the US Open on September 10.

2002 Americans Venus and Serena Williams become the first siblings to be ranked number one and number two in the world by the Women's Tennis Association.

2004 Roger Federer becomes the first male player since Mats Wilander in 1988 to win three Grand Slam events in a calendar year. Federer will dominate the sport for the next several years.

2008 Rafael Nadal breaks Federer's Wimbledon winning streak at five on July 6 with a five-set, five-hour win in the finals. Many believe it to be among the finest matches ever played.

LEGENDS OF TENNIS

Björn Borg
Sweden

Jack Kramer
United States

Rafael Nadal
Spain

Don Budge
United States

Rod Laver
Australia

William and Ernest Renshaw
England

Jimmy Connors
United States

Ivan Lendl
Czechoslovakia

Pete Sampras
United States

Roger Federer
Switzerland

John McEnroe
United States

Bill Tilden
United States

WOMEN

Maureen Connolly
United States

Steffi Graf
Germany

Martina Navratilova
Czechoslovakia

Margaret Smith Court
Australia

Billie Jean King
United State

Serena Williams
United States

Chris Evert
United States

Suzanne Lenglen
France

Venus Williams
United States

Althea Gibson
United States

Alice Marble
United States

Helen Wills Moody
United States

GLOSSARY

approach
A shot made by a player coming up to the net.

backhand
A stroke from the side of the body of the hand not holding the racket.

break
To win a game on an opponent's serve.

drop shot
The placement of a ball softly just over the net to make it hard for an opponent to reach it.

forehand
A stroke from the side of the body of the hand gripping the racket.

Grand Slam
The top four events in tennis—the Australian Open, the French Open, Wimbledon, and the US Open.

lob
An arching shot intended to be placed over the head and behind an opponent at the net.

match point
The point of a match in which a player can clinch a victory if he or she wins.

overhead
A hard slam shot on a ball over one's head, generally hit from near the net.

rally
A series of ground strokes from one player to the other.

serve
The shot that starts every point; it is tossed into the air and struck on the fly.

set
Part of a match that generally ends when one player wins six games. Victories in two or three sets result in the winning of a match.

tiebreaker
A series of points played to determine the winner of a set that ends in a 6–6 tie.

volley
A shot hit on the fly, generally at the net.

Selected Bibliography

Collins, Bud. *The Bud Collins History of Tennis*. Washington DC: New Chapter Press, 2010. Print.

"History of Tennis – Open Era." *Tennis Theme.com*. Tennistheme.com. n.d. Web. 22 Feb. 2011.

"History of Tennis – Origins of Tennis Game." *Tennis Theme.com*. Tennistheme.com. n.d. Web. 22 Feb. 2011.

McEnroe, John, and James Kaplan. *You Cannot Be Serious*. New York: G.P. Putnam's Sons, 2002. Print.

Roberts, Selena. *A Necessary Spectacle*. New York: Crown Publishing, 2005. Print.

Further Readings

Bradley, Michael. *On the Court With… Venus and Serena Williams*. Tarrytown, N.Y.: Marshall Cavendish Children's Books, 2005. Print.

Egart, Patricia. *Let's Play Tennis!* St. Paul, MN: Amber Skye Publishing, 2010. Print.

Sherrow, Victoria. *Tennis (History of Sports)*. San Diego, CA: Lucent Books, 2003. Print.

Web Links

To learn more about tennis, visit ABDO Publishing Company online at **www.abdopublishing.com**. Web sites about tennis are featured on our Book Links page. These links are routinely monitored and updated to provide the most current information available.

Places to Visit

International Tennis Hall of Fame Museum

194 Bellevue Avenue, Newport, RI 02840
(401) 849-3990
www.tennisfame.com
The museum chronicles more than eight centuries of tennis history through interactive exhibits, videos, and memorabilia. The grounds also feature 13 grass tennis courts.

United States Tennis Association Billie Jean King National Tennis Center

Flushing Meadows Corona Park, Flushing, NY 11368
(718) 760-6200
www.usta.com/About-USTA/National-Tennis-Center/National%20 Tennis%20Center/
The National Tennis Center, home to the US Open, is located in Flushing Meadows Corona Park. The Arthur Ashe Stadium is at the northern end of the park. Opened in 1997 and seating 23,000 fans, Arthur Ashe Stadium is the largest tennis stadium in the world.

INDEX

ABOUT THE AUTHOR

Marty Gitlin is a freelance writer based in Cleveland, Ohio. He has written more than 35 educational books. Gitlin has won more than 45 awards during his 25 years as a writer, including first place for general excellence from the Associated Press. He lives with his wife and three children.